EXPLORING DINOSAURS & PREHISTORIC CREATURES

AMMONOIDS

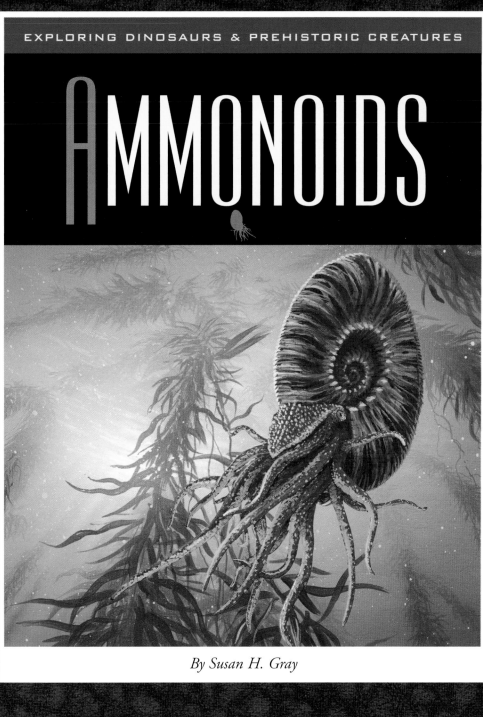

By Susan H. Gray

THE CHILD'S WORLD®
CHANHASSEN, MINNESOTA

Published in the United States of America by The Child's World®
PO Box 326, Chanhassen, MN 55317-0326
800-599-READ
www.childsworld.com

Content Adviser:
Brian Huber, PhD,
Curator, Department
of Paleobiology,
Smithsonian
National Museum
of Natural History,
Washington DC

Photo Credits: Illustration by Karen Carr: 5, 6; Jonathan Blair/Corbis: 10; Jeffrey L. Rotman/Corbis: 11, 12; Layne Kennedy/Corbis: 13, 14, 15; Stephen Frink/Corbis: 19; The Natural History Museum, London: 22, 23; Sinclair Stammers/Photo Researchers, Inc.: 7, 16; Chase Studio/Photo Researchers, Inc.: 8; British Antarctic Survey/Photo Researchers, Inc.: 9; Alfred Pasieka/Photo Researchers, Inc.: 20; Tom McHugh/Field Museum, Chicago/Photo Researchers, Inc.: 21, 24; Christian Jegou/Photo Researchers, Inc.: 25; Stephen J. Krasemann/Photo Researchers, Inc.: 26; David A. Hardy/Photo Researchers, Inc.: 27.

The Child's World®: Mary Berendes, Publishing Director

Editorial Directions, Inc.: E. Russell Primm, Editorial Director; Pam Rosenberg, Line Editor; Katie Marsico, Associate Editor; Matthew Messbarger, Editorial Assistant; Susan Hindman, Copy Editor; Melissa McDaniel, Proofreader; Tim Griffin/IndexServ, Indexer; Olivia Nellums, Fact Checker; Dawn Friedman, Photo Researcher; Linda S. Koutris, Photo Selector

Original cover art by Todd Marshall

The Design Lab: Kathleen Petelinsek, design; Kari Thornborough, page production

Library of Congress Cataloging-in-Publication Data
Gray, Susan Heinrichs.
  Ammonoids / by Susan H. Gray.
     p. cm. — (Exploring dinosaurs & prehistoric creatures)
  Includes index.
  ISBN 1-59296-407-9 (lib. bd. : alk. paper) 1. Ammonoidea—Juvenile literature.
I. Title.
  QE807.A5G73 2005
  564'.53—dc22   2004018069

Table of Contents

CHAPTER ONE

A Close Call

Deep in the ocean, the ammonoids (AM-uh-noydz) were swimming peacefully. It was cold and dark, with barely enough light to see. But that didn't bother the ammonoids. This was their home.

Suddenly, something passed by overhead. It was huge. A mosasaur (MOH-suh-sawr) was on the hunt. The fierce swimming **reptile** spotted the ammonoids and dove toward them, its toothy mouth wide open. The ammonoids began to scatter. A few swam with all their might, spewing jets of water from their bodies and shooting out of sight. Others drew quickly into their shells and sank to the seafloor.

The mosasaur thrashed to the right and left, trying desperately to grab one of the tasty ammonoids. But he stirred up the water so badly that he couldn't see what he was doing. Meanwhile, the ammonoids

silently escaped. That was a close call. They might not be so lucky the

next time.

A mosasaur tries to catch an ammonoid. The largest mosasaurs were nearly 57 feet (17 meters) long!

CHAPTER TWO

WHAT WERE AMMONOIDS?

Ammonoids were animals that lived in the oceans from about 400 million to 65 million years ago. An ammonoid had a soft body and **tentacles** and lived inside a shell attached to its body.

Ammonoids built shells of many different shapes, but each one was basically a tube with the animal living in a chamber at one end. The rest

An ammonoid swims near an Archelon, *an ancient sea turtle that was as large as a small car. The largest ammonoids could grow to be nearly 9 feet (3 m) in diameter.*

of the shell was a series of

empty chambers

separated by thin

walls. Ammonoid

fossils have lines

showing where the

walls once were.

These lines are called

sutures (SOO-churz).

A collection of ammonoid fossils shows the tightly coiled shell patterns found in many of these animals.

Many ammonoids built shells that were tightly coiled, like cinna-

mon rolls. Others created shells that were perfectly straight, slightly

curved, or bent into a triangle. Still others made shells that were straight

at one end and coiled or bent double at the other. While many ammo-

noid shells are the size of marbles, some are bigger than truck tires!

An ammonoid's soft body was packed inside the shell, but its head and tentacles stuck out. The animal used its tentacles to grasp food and move it toward the mouth. Beaklike jaws were centered in the cluster of tentacles and hidden from view.

Ammonoids probably swam the same way that squids and octopuses do. They took in water and then squirted it out through

Ammonoids probably swam backwards by taking in water and shooting it out in front of themselves. The force of the water moving forward moved the animals in the opposite direction.

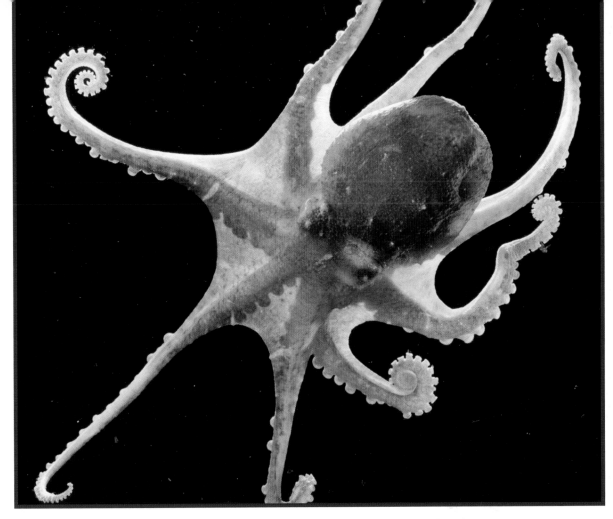

The Antarctic octopus (above) is a modern-day cephalopod.

a funnel at the front of the body. As the water shot forward, the

ammonoid jerked backward.

Ammonoids belonged to a large group of animals called the

cephalopods (SEFF-uh-luh-podz). Although the ammonoids have all

become **extinct,** many other cephalopods are still living today.

CHAPTER THREE

WHAT ARE CEPHALOPODS?

Cephalopods are ocean animals such as squids, octopuses, and nautiluses (NAW-tih-lus-ses). The word *cephalopod* comes from Greek words that mean "head foot." This refers to the many limbs attached to the head of the animal. More than 650 different

A nautilus can have more than 90 tentacles. These armlike structures are used for capturing prey.

A squid swims in the Red Sea. Squid are just one kind of cephalopod.

kinds of cephalopods are living today, and scientists have found about

7,500 different kinds that lived in the past.

The "feet" on the cephalopod's head are actually called arms, or

tentacles. The animals use them to crawl along the seafloor and to hold

food. The octopus has only 8 tentacles, but the nautilus may have

more than 90. It is likely that different kinds of ammonoids had

different numbers of tentacles.

Cephalopods are known to be very intelligent animals. They have large brains for their body size. Their large brains help them make complex, delicate movements. An octopus, for example, can pry shells apart and can even learn to unscrew jar lids.

Cephalopods are carnivores (KAR-nuh-vorz). This means they eat other animals for food. They are known to devour fish, worms, clams, shrimp, crabs, and other ocean creatures.

A giant Pacific octopus uses the suckers on its tentacles to hold on to the fish that will be its next meal.

SUCH SUTURES!

Every ammonoid started life as a very small animal, living in a little chamber within a tiny shell. As the creature grew and needed more space, it produced a substance that formed a newer, bigger chamber just beyond the one it was living in. The animal moved into this bigger chamber and then built a wall right behind its body. In doing this, the ammonoid sealed off the old chamber. As long as the ammonoid continued to grow, it kept on making new chambers and sealing off the old ones that were too small.

In ammonoid fossils, the chamber walls are usually hidden from view. However, suture lines on the outside of the fossil show their position. Sutures show that some ammonoids made chamber walls that were a little wavy. Other ammonoids created walls that

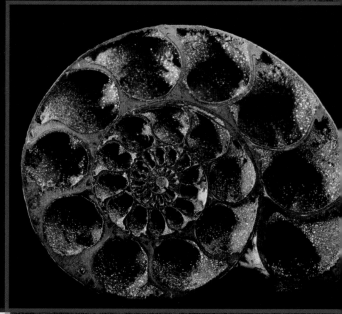

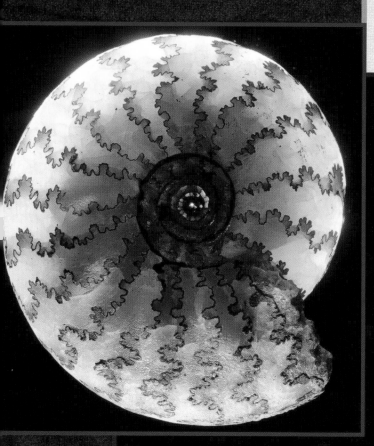

are wavy. This means that in the living ammonoid, the wall behind its body was wavy.

Ammonoids that lived more recently have more complicated sutures. These ceratitic (SEHR-uh-TIH-tik) sutures are wrinkled, with many S curves. The wall behind the living animal was wrinkled from top to bottom.

The most recent ammonoids have the most complex sutures of all. These ammonitic (AM-uh-NIH-tik) sutures have wrinkles on their wrinkles. In life, the wall behind the ammonoid's body was so folded, crinkled, and grooved, that it didn't even look like a wall.

were amazingly complicated. They had folds, grooves, wrinkles, and creases everywhere.

The earliest ammonoids built the simplest and plainest walls, and so have the simplest sutures. Scientists call this a goniatitic (GO-nee-uh-TIH-tik) pattern. Goniatitic sutures

CHAPTER FOUR

HOW DID AMMONOIDS
SPEND THEIR TIME?

To figure out how ammonoids spent their time, scientists

study their fossils and where they lived. Fossils show that

the youngest ammonoids were tiny. They must have been weak

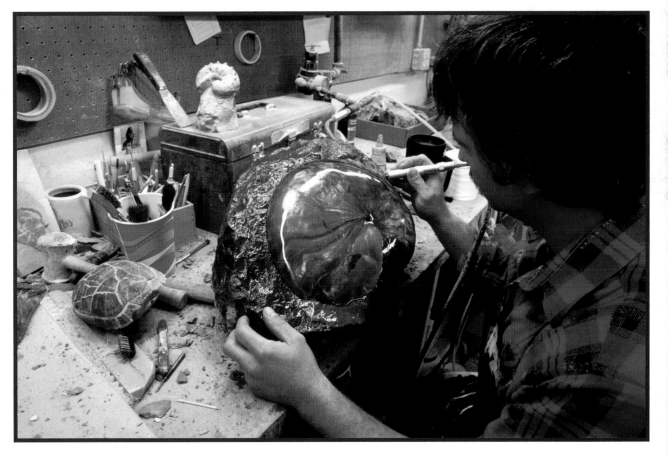

A scientist carefully works on an ammonoid fossil.

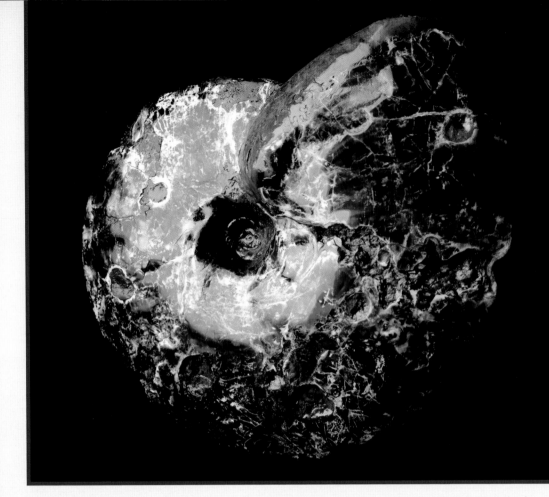

Can you see the bite marks on this fossil? Scientists know that ammonoids were food for other animals because some fossils have been found with bite marks on them.

swimmers that were pushed about by movements of the water. These

little ammonoids used their tentacles to grab and eat other small

animals that were floating along with them.

As the ammonoids grew, they ate larger and larger meals.

Scientists do not know exactly how they caught those meals. Perhaps the ammonoids became good swimmers and could catch fish or other ammonoids that were nearby. Perhaps the ammonoids simply floated along, grabbing whatever food came into their path. Perhaps they lived on the ocean floor, using their tentacles to creep about. There, they might have **preyed** on crabs and sea lilies, or eaten dead animals that had drifted down.

Ammonoids did not live in warm, shallow water. Instead, they preferred depths of 100 to 800 feet (31 to 246 m), where the water was relatively cool, still, and dark. They probably lived and traveled together in groups, like modern-day nautiluses and squids. This may have protected some from predators, but it didn't protect all of them. Large crabs and fish preyed on the ammonoids. Some ammonoid shells have mosasaur bite marks, which tells us that these reptiles fed on them as well.

The nautilus is the closest living relative of the ammonoids. This animal existed when ammonoids first appeared. It has changed little over its millions of years on Earth, and it is still around today. Scientists often call the nautilus a living fossil, and they study it to learn how ammonoids might have behaved.

Like many ammonoids, the nautilus lives in a coiled shell. As it grows, it moves into larger and larger chambers and seals off the smaller ones. It doesn't seal them off completely, however. Each chamber wall has a hole in the center. A tube of soft tissue extends from the animal's body through the series of holes. The nautilus can add or remove water from the chambers through this soft tube. By changing the amounts of water and air in its shell, the nautilus rises and sinks. Ammonoid shells have similar holes. Therefore, scientists believe that ammonoids—like the nautilus—could control how deeply they swam.

Like other cephalopods, the nautilus swims by jet propulsion, shooting water through a funnel near its head. By turning the funnel in different directions, the animal can move forward, backward, and sideways. If ammonoids had similar structures, they would have been able to steer quite well as they swam.

For protection, the nautilus pulls its head and tentacles inside its shell and draws down a hood to cover itself. Scientists have found ammonoid structures that look like trapdoors for closing up shell openings. So perhaps, instead of using a hood, the ammonoids clamped themselves shut inside their shells.

It's too bad that we have no living ammonoids to study. However, the nautilus can teach us much about how the ammonoids may have lived.

CHAPTER FIVE

MANY DIFFERENT AMMONOIDS

Scientists tell us that there were hundreds of different kinds of ammonoids. They **identify** an ammonoid by the shape of its shell and by its suture pattern. The ammonoid named *Goniatites*

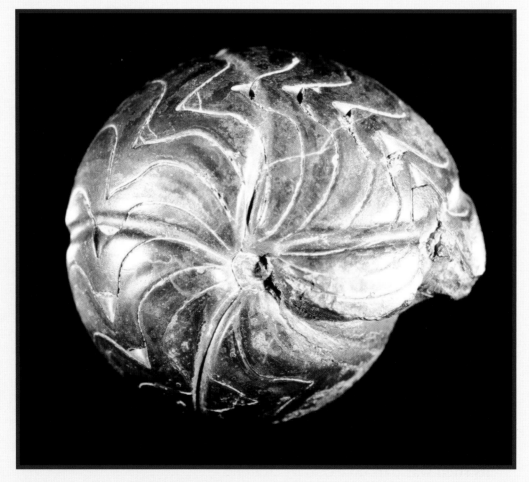

Goniatites *can be identified by its wavy sutures.*

(GO-nee-uh-TY-teez) had simple, wavy sutures and a wide, tightly coiled shell. The ammonoid named *Ceratites* (SEHR-uh-TY-teez) had more complex, S-shaped sutures. Can you guess what kind of sutures *Ammonites* (AM-uh-NY-teez) had?

Some Baculites *were several feet long.*

The ammonoid named *Baculites* (BAK-yoo-LY-teez) had very complex sutures with many folds, wrinkles, and creases. *Baculites* had a tightly coiled shell early in life. As it got older, it created new chambers in a straight line. So its shell was part coiled, part straight.

Hamulina (HAM-yoo-LY-nuh) grew a straight shell for much of its life. Then it made a U-turn and grew straight in the other direction.

One kind of *Hamites* (ham-MY-teez) built a shell that first grew straight, then doubled back on itself. For a while, it grew straight again, with many chambers in a straight line. Then it

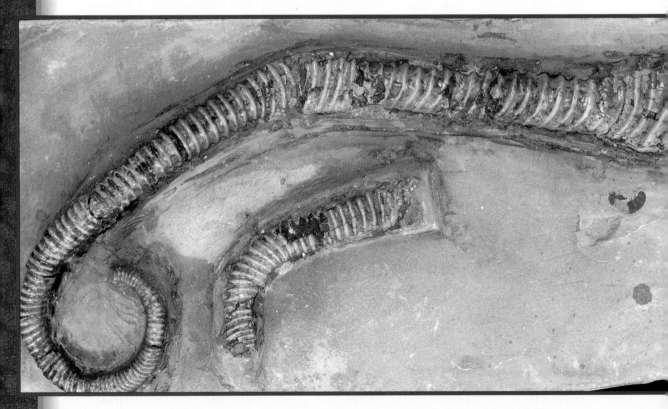

A Hamites *fossil demonstrates the unusual shape of the animal's shell.*

A Nipponites *shell may look like a tangled mess, but if you look closely, you can see that it is a series of connected U-shapes.*

doubled back again. The shell of this ammonoid wound up looking like a big paper clip!

Among the most unusual ammonoids was *Nipponites* (NIP-uh-NY-teez). It lived in seas that covered what is now Japan. Its shell did not grow into a spiral, but into a tangled mess. This ammonoid was probably a very poor swimmer that lived its whole life on the seafloor.

CHAPTER SIX

WHAT HAPPENED TO THE AMMONOIDS?

he oldest ammonoid fossils are about 400 million years old. This means that the ammonoids were here almost 200 million years before the first dinosaurs appeared.

By 367 million years ago, ammonoids were quite common. They shared Earth with many crawling and swimming animals and many **ancient** plants. However, something drastic took place at that time. Whatever it was, it wiped out millions of plants and animals. Scientists do not

The first ammonoids lived during a time known as the Devonian period. This period of Earth's history lasted from about 410 million years ago to about 360 million years ago.

know what happened to cause this mass extinction (ek-STINGKT-shuhn). But they do know that some ammonoids survived.

It took millions of years for Earth's plant and animal populations to build up again. During this time, the ammonoids increased and spread everywhere. Then, about 245 million years ago,

Ammonoids existed on Earth long before the first dinosaurs made their appearance.

The ammonoids survived three mass extinctions and were still around during the Cretaceous period (144 million to 65 million years ago). But when a fourth great extinction took place 65 million years ago, the ammonoids did not survive.

something happened again causing another mass extinction. This one was terrible, wiping out more than 90 percent of all plant and animal **species.** Amazingly, the ammonoids survived.

About 208 million years ago, there was yet another mass extinction. Although this one was not as great as the last, ocean and land animals still died out by the millions. Once again,

many tough little ammonoids made it

through.

Then, 65 million years

ago, one more mass extinc-

tion took place. Something

big happened that wiped out

every last dinosaur. It killed

the great flying reptiles of

the skies. It caused the fierce

Some scientists believe that the impact of a large asteroid hitting Earth may have caused the mass extinction that occurred 65 million years ago.

swimming reptiles of the oceans to disappear forever. It also wiped out

the mosasaurs—the predators of the ammonoids. But not even

the disappearance of their enemies could save the ammonoids this

time. After swimming the oceans for more than 300 million years, the

ammonoids were never seen again.

Glossary

ancient (AYN-shunt) Something that is ancient is very old; from thousands or even millions of years ago. Ammonoids were ancient cephalopods.

extinct (ek-STINGKT) Something that is extinct no longer exists. The ammonoids are extinct.

fossils (FOSS-uhls) A fossil is something left behind by an ancient plant or animal. Scientists learn about ammonoids by studying their fossils.

identify (eye-DEN-tuh-fye) To identify is to recognize and name. Scientists identify an ammonoid by the shape of its shell and by its suture pattern.

preyed (PRAYD) A creature that has preyed on something has hunted it down and eaten it. The mosasaur preyed on ammonoids.

reptile (REP-tile) A reptile is an air-breathing animal with a backbone and is usually covered with scales or plates. A mosasaur was an ancient swimming reptile.

species (SPEE-seez) Plants and animals are divided into species because of their common characteristics. More than 90 percent of all plant and animal species were wiped out about 245 million years ago.

tentacles (TEN-tuh-kuhls) Tentacles are long, flexible limbs found on some animals. The ammonoids used their tentacles to grasp food.

Did You Know?

▶ Ammonoids are named after the Egyptian god Ammon, who was believed to have curled horns on his head. The curled horns looked very much like the curled shells of the ammonoids.

▶ The shells of ammonoids were often decorated with knobs, ribs, and spines. These are not often preserved in their fossils.

▶ No one has found the fossilized tentacles of an ammonoid. Therefore, we do not know whether ammonoids had 10 tentacles or 100!

How to Learn More

AT THE LIBRARY

Blaxland, Beth. *Octopuses, Squids, and Their Relatives: Cephalopods.*
New York: Chelsea House Publications, 2002.

Woods, Samuel G. *Sorting Out Worms and Other Invertebrates: Everything You Want to Know about Insects, Corals, Mollusks, Sponges, and More!* Woodbridge, Conn.: Blackbirch Press, 1999.

ON THE WEB

Visit our home page for lots of links about ammonoids:

http://www.childsworld.com/links.html

NOTE TO PARENTS, TEACHERS, AND LIBRARIANS: We routinely verify our Web links to make sure they're safe, active sites—so encourage your readers to check them out!

PLACES TO VISIT OR CONTACT

AMERICAN MUSEUM OF NATURAL HISTORY
*To find out more about ammonoids
and other ancient animals*
Central Park West at 79th Street
New York, NY 10024-5192
212/769-5100

CARNEGIE MUSEUM OF NATURAL HISTORY
To view the fossils of many extinct animals
4400 Forbes Avenue
Pittsburgh, PA 15213
412/622-3131

MONTEREY BAY AQUARIUM
*To see living cephalopods and learn more
about these relatives of ammonoids*
886 Cannery Row
Monterey, CA 93940
831/648-4800

SMITHSONIAN NATIONAL MUSEUM OF NATURAL HISTORY
To see several fossil exhibits
10th Street and Constitution Avenue NW
Washington, DC 20560-0166
202/357-2700

The Geologic Time Scale

CAMBRIAN PERIOD

Date: 540 million to 505 million years ago
Most major animal groups appeared by the end of this period. Trilobites were common and algae became more diversified.

ORDOVICIAN PERIOD

Date: 505 million to 440 million years ago
Marine life became more diversified. Crinoids and blastoids appeared, as did corals and primitive fish. The first land plants appeared. The climate changed greatly during this period—it began as warm and moist, but temperatures ultimately dropped. Huge glaciers formed, causing sea levels to fall.

SILURIAN PERIOD

Date: 440 million to 410 million years ago
Glaciers melted, sea levels rose, and Earth's climate became more stable. Plants with vascular systems developed. This means they had parts that helped them conduct food and water.

DEVONIAN PERIOD

Date: 410 million to 360 million years ago
Fish became more diverse, as did land plants. The first trees and forests appeared at this time, and the earliest seed-bearing plants began to grow. The first land-living vertebrates and insects appeared. Fossils also reveal evidence of the first ammonoids and amphibians. The climate was warm and mild.

CARBONIFEROUS PERIOD

Date: 360 million to 286 million years ago
The climate was warm and humid, but cooled toward the end of the period. Coal swamps dotted the landscape, as did a multitude of ferns. The earliest reptiles appeared on Earth. Pelycosaurs such as *Edaphosaurus* evolved toward the end of the Carboniferous period.

PERMIAN PERIOD

Date: 286 million to 248 million years ago
Algae, sponges, and corals were common on the ocean floor. Amphibians and reptiles were also prevalent at this time, as were seed-bearing plants and conifers. However, this period ended with the largest mass extinction on Earth. This may have been caused by volcanic activity or the formation of glaciers and the lowering of sea levels.

TRIASSIC PERIOD

Date: 248 million to 208 million years ago
The climate during this period was warm and dry. The first true mammals appeared, as did frogs, salamanders, and lizards. Evergreen trees made up much of the plant life. The first dinosaurs, including *Coelophysis*, existed on Earth. In the skies, pterosaurs became the earliest winged reptiles to take flight. In the seas, ichthyosaurs and plesiosaurs made their appearance.

JURASSIC PERIOD

Date: 208 million to 144 million years ago

The climate of the Jurassic period was warm and moist. The first birds appeared at this time, and plant life was more diverse and widespread. Although dinosaurs didn't even exist in the beginning of the Triassic period, they ruled Earth by Jurassic times. *Allosaurus, Apatosaurus, Archaeopteryx, Brachiosaurus, Compsognathus, Diplodocus, Ichthyosaurus, Plesiosaurus,* and *Stegosaurus* were just a few of the prehistoric creatures that lived during this period.

CRETACEOUS PERIOD

Date: 144 million to 65 million years ago

The climate of the Cretaceous period was fairly mild. Many modern plants developed, including those with flowers. With flowering plants came a greater diversity of insect life. Birds further developed into two types: flying and flightless. Prehistoric creatures such as *Ankylosaurus, Edmontosaurus, Iguanodon, Maiasaura, Oviraptor, Psittacosaurus, Spinosaurus, Triceratops, Troodon, Tyrannosaurus rex,* and *Velociraptor* all existed during this period. At the end of the Cretaceous period came a great mass extinction that wiped out the dinosaurs, along with many other groups of animals.

TERTIARY PERIOD

Date: 65 million to 1.8 million years ago

Mammals were extremely diversified at this time, and modern-day creatures such as horses, dogs, cats, bears, and whales developed.

QUATERNARY PERIOD

Date: 1.8 million years ago to today

Temperatures continued to drop during this period. Several periods of glacial development led to what is known today as the Ice Age. Prehistoric creatures such as glyptodonts, mammoths, mastodons, *Megatherium,* and saber-toothed cats roamed Earth. A mass extinction of these animals occurred approximately 10,000 years ago. The first human beings evolved during the Quaternary period.

Index

About the Author

Susan H. Gray has bachelor's and master's degrees in zoology and has taught college-level courses in biology. She first fell in love with fossil hunting while studying paleontology in college. In her 25 years as an author, she has written many articles for scientists and researchers, and many science books for children. Susan enjoys gardening, traveling, and playing the piano. She and her husband, Michael, live in Cabot, Arkansas.